Nelson

Spelling

D1330434

Developing Skills

John Jackman

2

BOOK TWO

Scottish Adviser: Iain Campbell

CONTENTS/SCOPE AND SEQUENCE

Page	Focus	Extra	Extension	Focus resource	Extension resource
34/35 Unit 14 a al ad af	all or al	prefix meanings	using target prefixes	using al-	ad- af- al- a-word groups
36/37 Unit 15 f ff fe	using plurals	fe + s; f+ s	fe + ing/ed; f + ing/ed	f/ves plurals	-f -ff -fe plurals
38/39 Unit 16 en on endings	selecting en or on; cloze	en/on puzzle	adding en as suffix	-en -on word building	selecting -en -on endings
40/41 Unit 17 syllables	two-syllable words	multi-syllabic words	syllables/double consonants	2/3 syllable words	syllables in spelling
42/43 Unit 18 qu	q+u	qua puzzle	alphabetical order (3rd letter)	qu- fan (building)	alphabetical ordering (4th letter)
44/45 Unit 19 dge	spelling pattern families	dge + ing/ed	dge/ge	dge rhyming words; sorting -udge -edge -idge words	using -dge -age words
46/47 Check-up 2	Check-up 2	Check-up 2	Check-up 2	Check-up 2	Check-up 2
48/49 Unit 20 word roots	identifying roots	adding prefixes and suffixes	Latin and Greek origins	adding suffixes to roots	word webs diminutives
50/51 Unit 21 sion	word/picture matching	rhyming words	word/definition matching	-ision -usion -ension word building	making -sion abstract nouns
52/53 Unit 22 tion	word/picture matching	rhyming words	making abstract nouns	-action -ection -uction word building	making -tion abstract nouns
54/55 Unit 23 ive	word/picture matching	ive/sion	ive adjectives	-ive fan (building)	extended word families
56/57 Unit 24 able ible	cloze	able or ible?	e + able/ible	-able -ible patterns/ word building	adding -able/-ably and -ible/-ibly to roots
58/59 Unit 25 ough	word/picture matching	homophones	different ough sounds	-ough -ought patterns/word building	scrambled letter puzzle; ough homophones
60/61 Unit 26 wa	identifying wa words	wa words rhyming puzzle	contractions	wa- swa- patterns/ word building	using was want water wanted; contractions
62/64 Check-up 3	Check-up 3	Check-up 3	Check-up 3	Check-up 3	Check-up 3

OCUS

A Find the missing letters. Copy the words into your book.

1 d _____

2 d ___ s

3 _____ l

4 ___ d _

5 f ___

6 l _____

7 p _____

8 _ r _____

B What are these? Write the words into your book.

1

2

3

4

5

6

7

8

A Write the plural of these words.

1 girl   2 bus   3 wish   4 dress   5 play   6 factory

B Write the answers to these word sums.

1 talk + ing =   2 fly + ing =   3 trip + ing =
4 try + ed =   5 happy + ly =   6 beauty + ful =
7 slow + est =   8 smoke + y =   9 heavy + er =

C Write contractions for each of these pairs of words.

1 she is   2 is not   3 do not   4 there is   5 I have   6 they would

EXTENSION

A Write these sets of words in alphabetical order.

1 egg   extra   eat   essential

2 drive   deep   dance   division   dome

B Write these words correctly in your book, adding the missing silent letters.

1 __nock   2 s__ord   3 __onour

4 __our   5 __rite   6 com__

ea

Ready, steady, go!

FOCUS

KEY WORDS

dead
head
read
bread
tread
health
wealth
spread
feather
leather
weather
ready
steady
wealthy

A Look at the pictures.
Write the rhyming key words they give clues to.
The first one is done to help you.

1 **weather** rhymes with 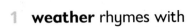 *feather*

2 **tread** rhymes with

3 **spread** rhymes with

4 **steady** rhymes with

5 **healthy** rhymes with

6 **dead** rhymes with

B Write five other **ea** words that sound like **e** in **bed**.

C Write the key word that can be said in more than one way.

Find and copy into your book twelve **ea** words hidden in the puzzle.

b	g	p	m	h	e	a	d	j
d	p	l	e	a	s	u	r	e
t	r	e	a	s	u	r	e	a
h	b	a	s	i	c	k	a	l
r	r	s	u	a	l	e	d	o
e	e	a	r	n	f	j	y	u
a	a	n	e	d	e	a	d	s
d	d	t	r	e	a	d	h	m

XTENSION

Remember, **homophones** have a similar sound but different spelling and meaning.

Sometimes **ea** can make the sound of **a** as in **make**, like this:

br**ea**k   gr**ea**t   st**ea**k

A Complete these word webs, adding as many prefixes and suffixes or both, to see how many family words you can find.

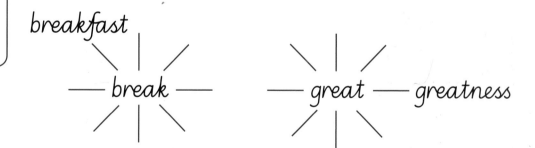

breakfast

break

great — greatness

B Copy the three **ea** words from the box. Next to each one write a homophone. Write a fun sentence for each pair of homophones.

ask
ast
ass

We made a vast number of masks in class!

KEY WORDS

ask
mask
flask
cast
fast
last
past
vast
blast
disaster
pass
class
glass
grass

A Copy these groups of words.
Underline the one with the different letter pattern.

1 ask   mask   past   flask   task

2 last   fast   class   vast   disaster

3 pass   class   grass   glass   mask

B Find ten **ask**, **ast** or **ass** words hidden in the puzzle box. Copy them into your book.

p	m	g	l	a	s	s	f
c	a	s	k	e	g	t	a
h	s	i	e	l	r	a	s
y	t	o	m	p	a	s	t
e	c	l	a	s	s	k	c
p	a	s	s	o	s	t	x
l	p	t	k	z	m	n	k

C Write a sentence using two of the words you have found.

Find a key word to match each clue.

1   container for liquids   fl_____

2   worn on the face   m_____

3   quickly   f_____

4   huge   v_____

5   explosion   bl_____

6   group of school children   cl_____

7   green plant   gr_____

8   used in windows   gl_____

EXTENSION

> Remember, if we need to make a noun plural, we usually just add **s**, like this:
>
> mask   mask**s**   blast   blast**s**
>
> But if the word already ends in **s** or **ss**, we add **es**, like this:
>
> bus   bus**es**   pass   pass**es**

Plural means more than one.

A Copy these words into your book and then write each word again adding **s** or **es**.

1 task   2 class   3 last   4 mast

5 glass   6 blast   7 master   8 brass

9 disaster   10 grass   11 mask   12 flask

B Why do you think that we add **es** and not just **s** to words that end in **s** or **ss**?

ur
ure

Blow, blow, blow the bubble mix**ture**.
Blow, till the bubble b**ur**sts!

 **OCUS**

 KEY WORDS

burn
turn
curl
hurt
nurse
purse
curve
burst
church

measure
treasure
picture
adventure

How many key words can you find in this picture?
Write the words in your book.

Write some sentences about the picture, using as many key words as
you can.

Sometimes there can be two **ur** sounds in a word, but made by different letter patterns.

b**ur**n**er**   advent**urer**

A Copy the words in the box, underlining the two **ur** sounds in each one.

curler   purser   lecturer   torturer
dirtier   measurer   firmer   surgery

B Write a fun sentence that includes at least four of these words.

XTENSION

v	s	e	m	b	u	r	n
f	u	r	e	y	p	x	g
t	r	e	a	s	u	r	e
u	f	t	s	u	r	h	h
r	n	n	u	r	s	e	u
n	r	s	r	e	e	l	r
o	x	p	e	c	u	r	l

Think whether you need to drop the final **e** before adding **ing**.

A Hidden in the puzzle box are eleven different **ur** words. Copy them into your book.

B Add **ing** to four of the words and write sentences using your new words.

ing
ed

washed

washing

FOCUS

KEY WORDS

cooking
washing
marrying
spying
shopping
hugging
dragging
dropping
waving
smiling
skating
exploring

Choose a verb ending in **ing** from the key words to match each picture.

Write about what happens to **shop**, **hug** and **drag** when **ing** is added?

EXTRA

Remember, the vowel letters are **a**, **e**, **i**, **o** and **u**. The other letters are consonants.

Remember to add **ing** or **ed** to a short word, look at the letter before the last letter.
If it is a **consonant**, just add **ing**.
If it is a **single vowel**, double the last letter and add **ing** or **ed**.
But, if there are **two vowels** together, just add **ing** or **ed**.

hop	hop**p**ing	sing	sing**ing**	re**a**d	rea**ding**
single vowel		consonant		two vowels together	
fit	fi**tt**ed	dump	dump**ed**	so**a**k	soak**ed**

For words ending in **w**, **x** or **y**, don't double the last letter.

play   play**ing**   play**ed**

Add **ing** and **ed** to each of these verbs.

1 clap	2 tug	3 nod	4 slip
5 strap	6 stoop	7 screw	8 munch
9 saw	10 bang	11 fill	12 relax

EXTENSION

Remember, to add **ing** or **ed** to a word that ends with **e**, we normally remove the **e** first.

shav**e**   shaving   shaved

A Add **ing** and **ed** to each of these words.

1 chase	2 dive	3 poke	4 close
5 stroke	6 tune	7 save	8 blame
9 choke	10 rule	11 behave	12 shave

B Write five more verbs that end in **e** and add **ing** and **ed**.

double consonants

I had a little kitten last summer.
The kitten was as little as my hand.
But the kitten isn't little any longer.
I just don't understand!

FOCUS

KEY WORDS

happy
rabbit

tennis

messy

silly

kitten

potter

coffee

summer

puppy

Write a key word to match each picture.
Underline the vowel letter (**a**, **e**, **i**, **o**, **u**) before the double letters.

1

2

3

4

5

6

Read the words. Write what you notice about the sound the vowel
letter before the double letters makes.

A Copy these pairs of words into your book.
Write about what you notice.

hopping   hoping   supper   super   written   writing

comma   coma   dinner   diner   tapping   taping

All your answers must
have double letters.

B What am I?

1 I'm a common fruit, beginning with **a**.
2 I'm a young dog.
3 You put your head on me in bed.
4 I'm usually in a pot next to the salt.
5 I'm a young cat.
6 You boil water in me.
7 I'm collected from flowers by bees.
8 I'm an animal with long ears.

XTENSION

Make a double letter alphabet, like this:

gra**bb**ed   su**cc**ess   pu**dd**ing

There are seven consonant letters that we never double.
Can you decide which ones these are?

ness
ment

enjoyment

happiness

darkness

laziness

silliness

OCUS

KEY WORDS

darkness
fitness
illness
likeness
weakness

happiness
laziness
silliness
ugliness

agreement
department
enjoyment
statement

A Write the key word to go with each picture.

B Look at these words.

ill   enjoy   agree   quiet   treat   bright
pay   fit   state   dark   punish

You can add **ness** to some, and you can add **ment** to others.
Make two lists, one for each type.

EXTRA

Listen carefully to the sound of the **y** before deciding whether to change it!

Remember, to add a suffix to a word that ends in **y**, where the **y** sounds like **i** in t<u>i</u>n, change the **y** to an **i** and add the suffix, like this:
ug**ly** ug**li**ness   mer**ry** mer**ri**ment

Add **ness** or **ment** to each of these words and then use four of the new words in sentences.

1 *lazy*	2 *naughty*	3 *nasty*	4 *empty*
5 *enjoy*	6 *pay*	7 *happy*	8 *heavy*
9 *dry*	10 *pretty*	11 *silly*	12 *employ*

EXTENSION

When trying to remember a difficult word it sometimes helps to look for a smaller word inside the bigger one.

Necessary is a difficult word to spell until you remember it has a **cess** pit in the middle of it (a cess pit is where sewage is pumped if there is no main drainage!).

Here are some more **cess** words.

> *excessive   recess   procession   abscess*
> *unnecessary   concession   successful*

Copy the words, then put each of them into a sentence to show what it means. Use a dictionary to help you.

silent letters

FOCUS

KEY WORDS

bomb
climb
thumb
kneel
knew
knock
wrinkle
write
answer
sword
school
gnat
design
scissors

A Look at these picture clues.
Write the key words in your book.

1 b_____

2 g_____

3 t_____

4 c_____

5 w_____

6 s_____

7 k_____

8 s_____

9 s_____

B Underline the letters you do not hear or say when they are read aloud.

EXTRA

Silent letters often have another particular letter next to them.
write   **wr**ong   **wr**inkle

A Write a sentence to say what you notice about the consonant letters close to the silent letters in each of these groups of words?

1 wrestle wrapper wreck
2 gnome gnaw resign
3 lamb numb climber
4 scent scenery scissors
5 debt doubt subtle
6 knuckle knock knight
7 castle bustle listen rustle

B Write as many words as you can to add to each of the word groups in A.

EXTENSION

Check your answers in a dictionary.

Write each of these groups of words in alphabetical order.

1 *lamb   thumb   bomber   crumble*
2 *gnat   gnome   gnash   gnaw*
3 *knee   knelt   kneel   knew*
4 *write   wrong   wrapper   wrath*
5 *climb   comb   crumb   climbing*

ship
hood

knight**hood**

champion**ship**

FOCUS

KEY WORDS

membership
partnership
ownership
workmanship
championship
craftsmanship

childhood
knighthood
motherhood
fatherhood
neighbourhood
falsehood

Look at these words.

mother   member   neighbour   child champion   workman   owner false   knight   partner

Some you can add **ship** to and some you can add **hood** to.
Make two lists, one for each type.

Write two sentences, using at least one word from each list.

EXTRA

Remember, a **suffix** is a group of letters added to the end of a word.

Copy these words into your book. Neatly underline the suffix in one colour and the root word to which it is fixed in another colour.

1 neighbourhood
2 friendship
3 fellowship
4 parenthood
5 adulthood
6 dictatorship
7 apprenticeship
8 priesthood

EXTENSION

These words have other suffixes. Some have more than one suffix. Copy the words and next to each write the suffix or suffixes. The first one is done to help you.

1 worthlessness   less   ness
2 carelessness
3 replaceable
4 movement
5 foolishness
6 interestingly
7 temptation

al
ary

hospit**al**   libr**ary**

HOSPITAL

pedal

metal

petal

sandal

FOCUS

KEY WORDS

capital
pedal
petal
sandal
signal
hospital
accidental
special
usual
occasional
dictionary
library
anniversary
necessary

A Match a key word to each of these pictures.
Write the answers in your book.

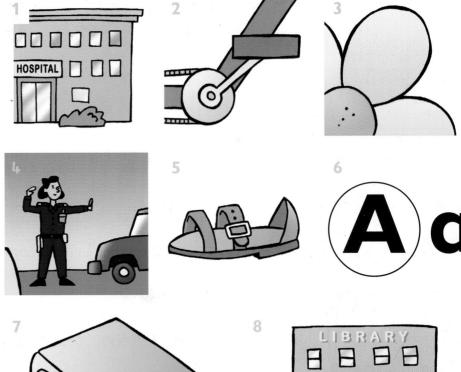

1 HOSPITAL

2

3

4

5

6 **A a**

7

8 LIBRARY

B Write a sentence about three of the pictures.

22

Remember, **adjectives** describe nouns.

Many words that end in **al** are adjectives.
For example: dentist (noun)   dental (adjective)

A For each of these nouns, write the related adjective by adding the **al** suffix.
Check your answers in a dictionary.

1 nature   2 topic   3 medicine   4 centre   5 music

6 norm   7 accident   8 bride   9 comic   10 mechanic

B For each of these adjectives, write the related noun.

1 occasional   2 signal   3 original   4 factual   5 historical

XTENSION

Use a dictionary to check your answers.

Many adverbs end in **ly**. When adding the **ly** suffix to a word ending in **al** don't be tempted to drop an **l**. You need them both!

A Copy and finish this chart.

noun	adjective	adverb
norm	normal	normally
nation		
origin		
accident		
act	actual	
event		

B What do you notice about the last two?

homophones

Can you **see** the **sea**?

KEY WORDS

be
bee
new
knew
there
their
for
four
hole
whole
right
write

Remember, **homophones** are words that sound the same but are spelt differently and have different meanings.
I paid **four** pounds **for** Mum's flowers.

Copy these words and write a homophone next to each one.
The first one has been done to help you.

1 threw   *through*

2 write   3 new   4 there   5 hole

6 right   7 place   8 great   9 mite

10 know

EXTRA

Homo means *same* and **phone** means *sound*.

Copy these sentences choosing the correct word from the homophones.

1 Have you scene/seen my basketball?

2 No/Know, where/wear did you last sea/see it?

3 I/Eye am knot/not sure/shore weather/whether it was won/one or to/two/too daze/days ago.

EXTENSION

Homonyms are similar to homophones. **Homonyms** have the same sound and the same spelling but different meanings.

bank   a place to keep money
bank   the edge of a river

A Copy these words and write two definitions for each. You may need a dictionary to help you.

1 bark   2 club   3 hatch   4 rush

5 watch   6 arms   7 down   8 sink

B Make a list of other homonyms. Use each of them in sentences to show their different meanings.

OCUS

A What are these? The letters will give you a clue.
Write the words in your book.

1 b_____   2 f_____   3 ____sk   4 __i_____

5 p_____   6 __a____   7 __n_____   8 s_____

9 s_____   10 ____d____   11 s__g____   12 l_____

B Write a fun sentence that includes four of the words from A.

EXTRA

A Copy these words into your book and next to each write the word again adding **s** or **es**.

1 flask   2 class   3 blast   4 disaster   5 glass

B Copy these words into your book and underline the two **ur** sounds in each one.

1 curler   2 lecturer   3 torturer   4 surgery

C Add **ing** and **ed** to each of these verbs.

1 slap   2 saw   3 nod   4 slip   5 strap   6 relax

D Add **ness** or **ment** to each of these words.

1 happy   2 naughty   3 enjoy   4 lazy   5 nasty   6 pay

E Write a sentence to say what you notice about the letters close to the silent letters in these words?

1 wrestle wrapper wreck   2 lamb numb climber   3 debt doubt subtle

F Copy these words and write a homophone next to each one.

1 right   2 great   3 new   4 there   5 hole

EXTENSION

A Add **ing** and **ed** to each of these words.

1 close   2 dive   3 stroke   4 blame   5 choke

B Write each of these groups of words in alphabetical order.

1 lamb   crumb   climb   bomb

2 gnat   gnome   gnash   gnaw

3 knee   knew   knelt

C Copy the words and next to each write the suffix or suffixes.

1 motherhood   2 carelessness   3 championship

4 foolishness   5 inspection   6 interestingly

dictionary work

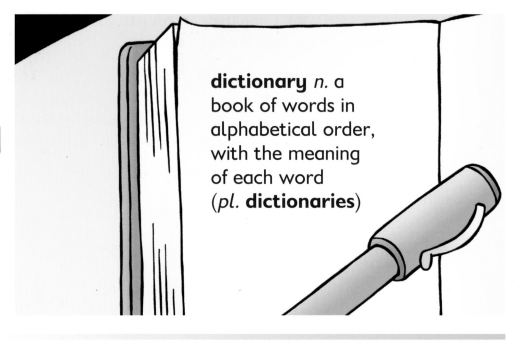

dictionary *n.* a book of words in alphabetical order, with the meaning of each word (*pl.* **dictionaries**)

KEY WORDS

letter
order
dictionary

vowel
consonant

alphabet
alphabetical

definition

first
last
between

a b c d e f g h i j k l m n o p q r s t u v w x y z

Remember, there are 26 letters in the alphabet.
Five of these are the **vowels a**, **e**, **i**, **o** and **u**.
The other letters are called **consonants**.

Write the answers to these questions in your book. What is:

1 the first vowel?

2 the last consonant?

3 the vowel letter after **h**?

4 the consonant after **o**?

5 the letter before **r**?

6 the middle vowel letter?

7 Which consonant comes first, **m** or **n**?

8 Which comes first, **s** or **v**?

9 Which letter is between **k** and **m**?

10 Which letter is midway between **a** and **e**?

11 Is **p** nearer to **g** or **z**?

12 Is **n** nearer to **f** or **s**?

13 Which are the two vowel letters not found in **alphabetical**?

14 List the letters that are in the second half of the alphabet.

Remember, **alphabetical order** means the letters are put in the order of the letters in the alphabet.

The words in a dictionary are in alphabetical order.

Remember, if we are sorting words into alphabetical order, and they begin with the same letter, we need to use the second letter in each word.

lace   lettuce   lime   lottery   lunar

(a) b c d (e) f g h (i) j k l m n (o) p q r s t (u) v w x y z

If the second letters are the same we need to look at the third letters.

shark   sheep   shield   shoal   shriek

(a) b c d (e) f g h (i) j k l m n (o) p q (r) s t u v w x y z

A Write these words in alphabetical order. You will need to look at the second letters.

1 cud   cross   breed   commit   chair

2 fine   feud   fable   flexible

3 mould   measles   magistrate   muffle

B Write these words in alphabetical order. You will need to look at the third letters.

1 nurse   nun   nut   number

2 fowl   four   forecast   fossil

3 curtain   cupboard   custody   cutlass

E XTENSION

A **definition** is a meaning of a word.

A Write your own short definition for each of these words. The first one is done to help you.

1 luscious   sweet and delicious

2 explosive   3 motto   4 efficient

5 atmosphere   6 crystal   7 impossible

B Use a dictionary to find the definitions of the words in A. Copy them into your book.

igh

When the storm crashes and the **ligh**tning flashes,
the **high**wayman comes out at n**igh**t.

FOCUS

KEY WORDS

high
higher
height
sighed
sighing

mighty
mightily
nightie
tighten

lightning
flight

righteous
brightly
frightening

A Look at these picture clues.
Write an **igh** word for each in your book.

1 n _____

2 fl _____

3 t _____

4 l _____

B Copy all of the key words into your book. Carefully underline the
suffix or suffixes in each one.

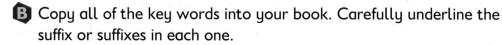

Use a dictionary to help you.

Root words with **igh** can often have suffixes and prefixes attached to them. Make a list of the words that can be made from these root words. The first one is done to help you.

1 *light*   *lights*   *lighting*   *lighter*   *lighten*
    enlighten   *lightening*   *lightning*

2 *bright*   3 *fright*   4 *high*

5 *might*   6 *right*   7 *sight*

Don't forget the **capital letters** and **full stops**!

Use a dictionary to help you answer these questions. Write a sentence for each answer.

1 What is the difference in meaning between **lightning** and **lightening**?

2 What does **enlighten** mean?

3 When would you use the word **mightier** and when would you use the word **mightiest**?

4 What do we mean when we say someone is **righteous**?

ous
ious

'Cur**ious**er and cur**ious**er!' cried Alice.

Alice in Wonderland Lewis Carroll

KEY WORDS

dangerous
enormous
famous
generous
jealous
nervous

curious
furious
previous
serious
various
victorious

Copy these sentences into your book. Fill the gaps with words from the key word list.

1 I really would like to be a f_____ racing driver.

2 It might be d_____, but it would be exciting.

3 My family would be n_____ as they watched me.

4 They would be proud if I was the v_____ driver and won the World Championship!

EXTRA

Remember, **adjectives** describe nouns.

A Match these adjectives with their nouns.
Write them in pairs in your book.

nouns	adjectives
danger	suspicious
jealousy	victorious
victory	nervous
nerve	disastrous
disaster	jealous
suspicion	dangerous

B Add at least another four pairs to your list.

EXTENSION

When adding the suffix **ous** or **ious** to words ending with **our**, first drop the **u** in the word to which the suffix is added, like this:

vapou̶r̶   vapor**ous**

A Add **ous** or **ious** to each of these words and then use each one in a sentence that shows its meaning.

1 victor   2 labour   3 vigour   4 glamour

B Some **ious** words can be particularly tricky.
Copy these into your book and underline the letter **i** in each.
Write out three times any that you think you might forget!

curious   vicious   anxious   conscious   precious   delicious
religious   suspicious   cautious   gracious

Now ask a friend to test you.

a al
ad
af

Asleep **a**float
a boat.

KEY WORDS

asleep
afloat
ablaze
aground
almost
already
always
although
adverb
adjust
advance
affect
affection
affluent

Remember, a **prefix** is a letter or group of letters at the beginning of a word.

When we use **all** at the beginning of a word, we always drop one **l**.

all + ways = always

A Copy and complete these word sums in your book.

1 all + most =   2 all + ready =

3 all + though =   4 all + so =

5 all + mighty =   6 all + together =

B Write a sentence that includes at least three **al** words.

XTRA

All right is always **two** words!

Use a dictionary to help you with the definitions.

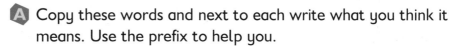

Prefixes have meanings.

al	means **all**	always
ad and **af**	mean **towards** or **tending towards**	advance affection
a	means **on** or **in**	aboard

A Copy these words and next to each write what you think it means. Use the prefix to help you.

1 *admire*   2 *almighty*   3 *affluent*

4 *asleep*   5 *adjoin*   6 *altogether*

7 *afflict*   8 *aground*   9 *affable*

B Copy the keys words with each of these prefixes and then use a dictionary to help you list three other words in each group.

1 *a*   2 *al*   3 *ad*   4 *af*

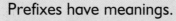XTENSION

Write a short story about a sea adventure, using as many **a**, **al**, **ad** and **af** words as you can. Try to keep your story to about 100 words or so. The picture will help you.

f ff
fe

Where are the wolves on the cliffs?

KEY WORDS

calf
calves
half
halves
loaf
loaves

cliff
cliffs
puff
puffs

knife
knives
wife
wives

Write a phrase to describe each of these pictures.
The first one is done to help you.

loaf

1 a basket of loaves

wolf

2 three _____

half

3 two _____

calf

4 new-born _____

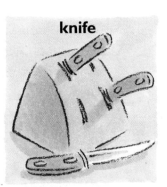

knife

5 three sharp _____

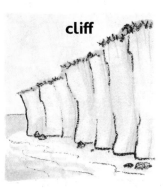

cliff

6 white _____

XTRA

For words ending in **ff**, just add **s** to make them plural.

To add a suffix to words ending in **f** or **fe**, we usually change the **f** or **fe** to **v** before adding the suffix, like this:

wi**f**e + s = wi**v**es   lea**f** + s = lea**v**es

A Copy this table of singulars and plurals and fill in the blanks.

singular	plural
half	
elf	
shelf	
wife	
life	
	sniffs
	selves

B Use a dictionary to find the plural of **chief** and **belief**. What do you notice?

XTENSION

When we add the suffixes **ing** and **ed** to words ending in **f** or **fe**, the same rules usually apply, but not always!
Complete each of these word sums, but use a dictionary to check your answers.

1 half + ed =

2 stuff + ing =

3 knife + ed =

4 thief + ing =

5 sniff + ing =

6 shelf + ed =

7 loaf + ing =

8 belief + ing =

9 puff + ing =

en on
endings

What happ**en**s when sev**en** little
kitt**en**s play with string and butt**on**s?

A mess!

FOCUS

KEY WORDS

oven
seven
kitten
siren
given
fatten
sudden
button
lesson
person
skeleton
lemon
season
poison

A Find the missing letters and copy the words into your book.
What do you notice about all the missing letters?

1 s__v__n   2 s__r__n   3 __v__n

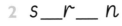  

4 b__tt__n   5 l__m__n   6 sk__l__t__n

B Copy these sentences into your book.
Fill each gap with a key word.

1 Suzie was_____ a special present.

2 It was a little_____ from the animal
rescue centre.

3 "It looks thin," said Suzie. "I will feed it lots
to_____ it up."

Find and write an **en** or **on** word to match each definition.

1 one more than six   _____ *en*

2 fastens clothes   _____ *on*

3 a young cat   _____ *en*

4 bones of the body   _____ *on*

5 type of glove   _____ *en*

6 can kill   _____ *on*

7 warning hooter   _____ *en*

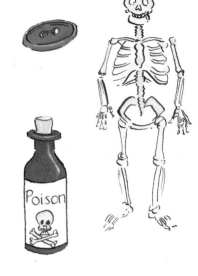

EXTENSION

Most words that end in **on** are nouns, like these:

     butt**on**   skelet**on**   pois**on**

en is often added to words to make them adjectives or verbs, like this:

     gold   gold**en**   weak   weak**en**   fat   fat**ten**

A Add **en** or **n** to each word in the box.
Sort them into three lists.
The first ones are done to help you.

gold	fat	give	short	flat	damp	fall
rot	woke	spoke	wood	bit	hid	take

+ en	double last letter + en	+ n
golden	fatten	given

B 1 Can you work out when you double the last letter before adding **en**? Can you work out when you just add **n**?

2 Write the rules in your book.

syllables

ti/ger

duck

kan/gar/oo

el/e/phant

hip/po/po/ta/mus

FOCUS

KEY WORDS

balloon
before
birthday
children
during
garden
happy
money

animals
different
following
important
suddenly
together

Remember, words have beats, like music has beats.

Say the key words out loud. Listen carefully for the beats in each word. Each beat is called a **syllable**.

Write the key words in your book.
Put a line between the syllables. The first one is done to help you.

1 *balloon*   bal / loon

Syllables are the sounds that make up a word. Each syllable makes a sound of its own. All syllables contain a vowel sound.

window is pronounced **w<u>i</u>n** / **d<u>o</u>w**   It has two syllables.

The two vowel sounds are underlined.

Make a table in your book like the one below. Write each word from the box under the correct heading.

one syllable	two syllables	three syllables	four syllables

year usually why woken those different unhappy
sure walking still near altogether started
disappointed paper uncertain sometimes often

EXTENSION

When words have double consonants, we usually split the syllables between the double letters.

swallow   swal / low

Write a rhyming two-syllable word for each of these words. Then mark the syllables in each word. The first one is done to help you.

1 middle *fid / dle*

2 rattle   3 hollow   4 sparrow 5 mutton

6 kitten   7 willow   8 muddle 9 happy

qu

Quick! Quack, quack!
Quiet! Quack, quack,
quack ...

OCUS

KEY WORDS

quack
question
quiz
quilt
quick
queen
quite
quiet

square
squeak
squirrel

banquet
liquid

conquer

A Which key words do you think of when you look at these pictures? Write them in your book.

3

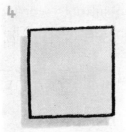

6

B Unscramble these **qu** words.

1 she wears a crown   e e u q n

2 not much noise   u i e q t

3 a puzzle   z i u q

4 needs an answer   s e t o n i u q

Find eleven **qua** words in the puzzle.
Write them into your book.

q	u	a	l	i	t	y	x	q	u	e	e
u	z	s	q	u	a	d	p	r	q	s	g
a	s	q	u	a	b	b	l	e	z	x	q
r	q	u	a	q	u	a	r	t	e	r	u
r	u	a	n	d	f	a	e	s	e	t	a
e	a	s	t	s	q	u	a	t	t	e	r
l	s	h	i	s	q	u	a	t	n	e	t
e	h	e	t	a	f	e	p	m	n	i	e
z	r	d	y	t	b	c	a	q	u	r	t

Read them quietly to yourself. What do you notice about the sound
the **a** makes in each word?

XTENSION

Remember, when we put words in alphabetical order, we first put
them in the order of their first letters. If the first letters are the
same, we then look at the second letters.

For example:
    screw   shrew   stew

If the first and second letters are the same, we must look at the
third letters, like this:

(a) b c d (e) f g h (i) j k l m n o p q r s t u v w x y z
qu**a**ck   qu**e**stion   qu**i**z

Careful!
The last one is tricky!

Write these groups of words in alphabetical order.

1 queen   quiet

2 quilt   quack

3 quite   quart   question

4 queen   quarter   quietly

5 quality   quickly   questions

6 quilt   quack   square

dge

The Billy Goats had to dodge the troll to cross the bridge.

 FOCUS

 KEY WORDS

badge
cadge
edge
hedge
ledge
bridge
fridge
ridge
dodge
lodge
lodger
fudge
judge

A Sort the key words into these families. Write them in your book.

adge   edge   idge   odge   udge

B How many words can you make by taking the first letter off **hedge** and adding something new?

For example: hedge   sledge

Now try the same thing with **judge**.

A Copy and finish this chart.

	+ ing	+ ed
cadge	cadging	cadged
hedge		
bridge		
dodge		
judge		

B Write a sentence about the picture on the page opposite using one of the **ing** words and another using a **d** word.

EXTENSION

Not all the words that have a **j** sound have the **dge** letter pattern. A **d** usually only goes before **ge** if it follows a short vowel sound, like this:

b**a**dge, fu**d**ge (short vowel, **d**)

p**a**ge, hu**g**e (long vowel, no **d**)

Beware! There are words with short vowels but no **d**, like these:

village   garage   college   allege

A Copy ten of the key words. Underline the short vowel in each one.

B Write these words in your book. Some need a **d** and others do not. Use a dictionary to help you.

1 crosses a river	bri_____	2 a row of bushes	he_____
3 a fruit	oran_____	4 keeps food cool	fri_____
5 gentle shove	nu_____	6 unusual	stran_____
7 strong anger	ra_____	8 a sign worn on clothes	ba_____

CHECK-UP 2

 **F**OCUS

A What are these? One letter is given to help you.
Write the words in your book.

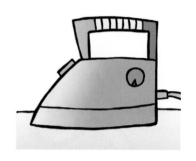

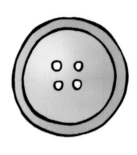

1 _____f

2 _____f

3 _u_____

4 i _____

5 _k_____

6 _e_____

7 s _____

8 _q_____

9 s _____

10 _a_____

11 _e _____

12 j _____

B Copy and complete these word sums in your book.

1 *all + most =*   2 *all + ready =*   3 *all + so =*

C Unscramble these **qu** words.

1 has four sides   *q s a r e u*

2 needs an answer   *s e t o u n i q*

46

A Sort these words into alphabetical order.

1 cod cone cot coast

2 hair half hard happen

B Make a list of the words that can be made from these root words.

1 light   2 fright   3 might

C Make an adjective ending with **ous** from each of these nouns.

1 danger 2 nerve 3 victory 4 suspicion

D Write the plural of these words.

1 half   2 wife   3 self   4 cliff   5 shelf

E 1 Write a one-syllable word.

2 Write a two-syllable word.

3 Write a three-syllable word.

EXTENSION

A Add **en** or **n** to each word to make another word from the same family.

1 gold   2 spoke   3 wood   4 flat   5 woke

B Write a rhyming two-syllable word for each of these words. Then mark the syllables in each word.

1 rattle 2 hollow 3 sparrow 4 muddle

C Write the answers to these clues in your book.

1 crosses a river   br _____

2 actors perform plays on this   st _____

3 a fruit   or _____

4 a sign worn on clothes   ba _____

5 gentle shove   nu _____

word roots

clean

cleanest

cleaning

cleaner

KEY WORDS

help
helping
helped
helper
helps
helpful
helpfully
helpless
unhelpful

graph
paragraph
autograph
photograph
geography
biography

A **root word** is a word to which **prefixes** and **suffixes** can be added to make other words in the same word family, like this:

clean   cleans **clean**ed un**clean   clean**ing **clean**er

Copy these pairs of words. Underline the root word, circle any prefixes in red and circle any suffixes in blue.

1 helping   unhelpful
2 photograph   paragraph
3 improve   improvement
4 bicycle   tricycle
5 unsure   surely
6 rider   override

Here are some useful prefixes and suffixes.

Prefixes:	un dis mis de re al

| Suffixes: | ly ful ed ing est er al |
| | ment ion ive ic ness ist |

Build as many words as you can based on these root words.

1 explore   2 art   3 like   4 cover   5 quick

XTENSION

Many root words came originally from other languages.

For example: **portare** is Latin for *to carry*, which has given us **porter**, **portable** and **report**.

Use a dictionary to help you discover words that have started from these roots. List them in your book.

1 decima (Latin for *a tenth*)

2 mikros (Greek for *small*)

3 ge (Greek for *earth*)

4 phone (Greek for *sound*)

5 scribere (Latin for *to write*)

6 navis (Latin for *a ship*)

sion

I must do my revi**sion** for a test on divi**sion**. I must practise comprehen**sion** so no more televi**sion**!

FOCUS

KEY WORDS

vision
television
revision
division
invasion
occasion
version
diversion
excursion
pension
extension
comprehension

A Match a key word to each of these pictures. Write the answers in your book.

1 _____   2 _____   3 _____

4 _____   5 _____   6 _____

B Write sentences about three of the pictures.

XTRA

A Find two words that rhyme with each of these words.
Write them in your book.

1 version   2 television   3 pension

B Write a short passage of not more than three sentences.
Each sentence must include at least one of the key words.

XTENSION

Read the words in the box and the list of definitions. Then match each
word to its definition. The first one is done for you.

> *passion   compassion   discussion   concussion   percussion*
> *concession   permission   admission   possession   profession*

1 talking something over   *discussion*

2 pity, sympathy or mercy

3 a strong feeling, such as love or hate

4 something granted as part of a bargain

5 dazed feeling caused by a blow

6 freedom to do something

7 a noisy striking

8 having as one's own

9 an occupation requiring a lot of training

10 letting people enter

tion

Birthday Instructions

1 Turn in the direction of the toy station.
2 Go to the toy box.
3 Open it a fraction.
4 Find your present!

 F OCUS

 KEY WORDS

question
station
relation
education
action
fraction
attraction
election
section
direction
suction
destruction
instruction

Match a key word to each of the pictures.

1

2

3

4

5

6

7

8

9

*function   section   connection   attraction   direction
suction   junction   election   infection   objection   selection
destruction   subtraction   instruction*

A The words in the box all end with **ction**, but there are four rhyming groups. Write them in the four lists below. One group is much bigger than the other three.

function	*section*	*attraction*	*suction*

B Choose one word from each list and put it in a sentence.

E XTENSION

Notice that the final **e** is dropped before **tion** is added.

Abstract nouns name things we cannot see, touch, hear, taste or smell.

Abstract nouns are often made by adding **tion** or **sion** to a verb. If the verb ends with **ate**, the abstract noun will end with **tion**.

Examples: educate   education

The **shun** sound at the end of a word is nearly always spelt **tion**. Never spell it with **sh** except in **fashion** and **cushion**.

A Use a dictionary to help you make the abstract noun to go with each of these verbs.

1 celebrate   2 operate   3 create   4 calculate
5 situate   6 evaporate   7 inspire   8 express
9 discuss   10 prepare   11 circulate   12 observe

The last one is tricky! A dictionary might help.

B Write the verbs related to these abstract nouns.

1 imitation   2 opposition   3 direction   4 action
5 frustration   6 cultivation   7 separation   8 detention

ive

Massive cuts in store now. Exclusive offers at competitive prices.

FOCUS

KEY WORDS

massive
excessive
aggressive
decisive
explosive
exclusive
expensive

competitive
motive
active
attractive
captive
deceptive
inquisitive

A Match a key word to each of these pictures.
Write the answers in your book.

B Write sentences about three of the pictures.

The suffix **ive** is sometimes added to root words that can also have the **ion** suffix.

For example: explode   explosive   explosion

Copy this table into your book and fill in the gaps.

+ ive	+ ion
explosive	explosion
aggressive	
	decision
	exclusion
	competition
relative	
	action
attractive	
	deception

A Many **ive** words are adjectives and could be used to describe a person. Make a list of all the key words that could be used in this way.

B Write a brief definition of each of the words you have chosen. Check your definitions in a dictionary.

able
ible

My lov**able** old horse is feeding in the st**able**.

FOCUS

KEY WORDS

able
table
stable
vegetable
reasonable
miserable
lovable
horrible
incredible
invisible
possible
responsible
sensible
terrible

Copy these sentences. Choose a key word to fill each gap.

I was r_____ for feeding Flossy each morning. She would always nuzzle my arm when I fed her; she was such a l_____ old horse.

As I walked towards her s_____ I had a h_____ feeling. The door was swinging open.

It just didn't seem p_____ that anyone could have taken her – but she had gone! I felt t_____ .

But then I spotted her – in the middle of the v_____ plot! Dad would be MAD!

Antonyms are opposites.

There is no easy way to know when to use **able** or when to use **ible**. Many more words end in **able** than end in **ible** but you should always check in a dictionary if you can.

This tip will also help.

If the antonym of the word starts with **un** it is an **able** word, but if the antonym starts with **in**, **il** or **ir** it is probably an **ible** word, though it could be either.

Examples: **un**suit**able**   **ir**resist**ible**   **il**leg**ible**

A Add **able** or **ible** to finish these words.

1 irrespons_____   2 unwork_____

3 unmend_____   4 incred_____

5 unlov_____   6 unclean_____

7 invis_____   8 unreason_____

B Write three sentences, each using one of the words you have just made.

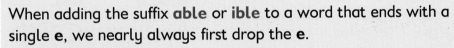

When adding the suffix **able** or **ible** to a word that ends with a single **e**, we nearly always first drop the **e**.

Example: valu~~e~~ + able = valuable

Do these word sums.

1 response + ible =   2 value + able =

3 cure + able =   4 desire + able =

5 believe + able =   6 recognise + able =

7 love + able =   8 sense + ible =

ough

The sea can be angry
The sea can be **rough**
The sea can be vicious
The sea can be **tough**.

John Foster

FOCUS

KEY WORDS

rough
enough

cough
trough

dough
though

nought
bought
brought
thought

bough
plough

Which key word does each picture remind you of?
Write them in your book.

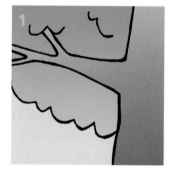

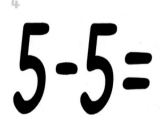

Remember, words like these are called **homophones**.

These sets of words have very similar sounds and so can cause spelling problems.

A Copy these sentences neatly into your book, selecting the correct words.

It was a rough/ruff morning. Boughs/Bows were falling from the trees, but the baker fort/fought his way to the village bakery. He knew his hot crusty bread was much sought/sort after by the tourists and no sooner had he started baking his first batch of doe/dough than he saw his first customers of the day peeping in threw/through his window.

B Use a dictionary to check your answers.

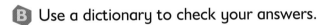

 XTENSION

A 1 Write two words where the **ough** sounds like the **uff** in **fluff**.
   2 Write two words where the **ough** sounds like **off**.
   3 Write two words where the **ough** sounds like the **ow** in **snow**.
   4 Write two words where the **ough** sounds like the **ow** in **how**.

B Beware! The letter pattern **augh** can sometimes make a similar sound to **ough** in **bought**, or sometimes it sounds like **ar** in **park**.

laughter   taught   caught   laugh   daughter
slaughter   laughing   naughty   draughts

Sort these nine words into two sets according to the sound made by the **augh** letter pattern.
Write a fun sentence using as many of the **augh** words as you can.

wa

Wanda!
Wash, Wanda!
Water, Wanda
- wash!
Warm water.
Wash!

OCUS

KEY WORDS

was

wasp

wash

want

wand

wander

water

watch

swan

swap

swamp

ward

warn

warm

A Find the **wa** words in the picture. Write them in your book.

B Draw a picture of something that begins with **swa**. Write its name.

EXTRA

Write a key word from the box opposite to answer these riddles.

1 a big white bird that rhymes with **gone**
2 not very hot and rhymes with **storm**
3 makes you clean and rhymes with **cosh**
4 a conjuror's stick, that rhymes with **pond**
5 to walk slowly, that rhymes with **ponder**

EXTENSION

Remember, sometimes we run words together as we speak.
This makes new words called **contractions**.
If we say **was** and **not** together they become **wasn't**.
The **apostrophe** (') shows where a letter or letters have been left out.

' is called an **apostrophe**.

A Here are some of the trickier contractions to spell.
What two words were put together to make these new words?
The first one is done for you.

1 *wouldn't* = would not

2 *can't*   3 *won't*   4 *I'd*   5 *shan't*

B How would you write these words if they were made shorter?
The first one is done for you.

1 *was not* = wasn't

2 *shall not* 3 *I would* 4 *can not* 5 *will not*

CHECK-UP 3

FOCUS

A What are these? The letters will give you a clue.
Write the words in your book.

1 f_____   2 _____k   3 c_____   4 __n____

5 s_____   6 __i_____   7 _____f   8 b_____

9 s_____   10 s_____   11 j_____   12 t_____

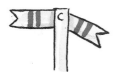  

13 d_____   14 __t_____   15 v_____   16 c_____

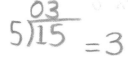   

17 __o_____   18 p_____   19 _____s__   20 w_____

B Copy these pairs of words. Underline the root, circle any prefixes in red and circle any suffixes in blue.

1 unkind   kindness   2 impossible   possibly

3 uncertain   certainly   4 precaution   cautionary

A Copy and complete these word sums in your book.

1 clap + ing =   2 slip + ed =   3 strap + ing =

4 enjoy + ment =   5 lazy + ness =   6 danger + ous =

7 victory + ous =   8 wife + s =   9 shelf + s =

10 blame + less =   11 choke + ing =   12 class + s =

13 all + ready =   14 all + ways =   15 all + together =

B Copy these words into your book, and underline the two **ur** sounds in each one.

1 surgery   2 lecturer

3 torturer   4 curler

C Copy these words and write a homophone next to each one.

1 new   2 through   3 right   4 lead

5 doe   6 bough   7 moor   8 two

9 hare   10 wear   11 here   12 no

D Build as many words as you can based on these root words.

1 help   2 explode   3 relate   4 believe

5 know   6 appoint   7 curl   8 joy

E Add **able** or **ible** to finish these words.

1 incred_____   2 unwork_____

3 unmend_____   4 irrespons_____

5 disagree_____   6 unaccept_____

A Write each of these groups of words in alphabetical order.

1 some   come   bomb   home

2 write   wrong   wrestle   whole

3 spice   spare   sport   spear

4 think   throw   thud   there

5 about   able   abroad   ability

6 draft   drift   drink   dredge

B Copy the words and next to each write the suffix or suffixes.

1 neighbourhood   2 thoughtlessness   3 craftsmanship

4 helplessness   5 childhood   6 disinterested

7 excessive   8 disappointing   9 irresponsible

C Add **en** or **n** to each word to make another word from the same family.

1 wood   2 awake   3 gold   4 flat   5 broke

6 damp   7 take   8 spoke   9 hid   10 short

D Write a rhyming two-syllable word for each of these words. Then mark the syllables in each word.

1 forgotten   2 borrow   3 narrow   4 puddle   5 riddle

6 battle   7 fellow   8 willow   9 brittle   10 funnel

E Use a dictionary to help you make the abstract noun to go with each of these verbs.

1 discuss   2 express   3 operate   4 calculate   5 observe